Caring for Your
Ferret

Lynn Hamilton

Weigl Publishers Inc.

Project Coordinator
Heather C. Hudak

Design and Layout
Warren Clark
Katherine Phillips

Copy Editor
Tina Schwartzenberger

Photo Research
Tracey Carruthers

Published by Weigl Publishers Inc.
350 5th Avenue, Suite 3304, PMB 6G
New York, NY 10118-0069 USA
Web site: www.weigl.com

Library of Congress Cataloging-in-Publication Data

Hamilton, Lynn A., 1964-
  Caring for your ferret / Lynn Hamilton.
      v. cm. -- (Caring for your pet)
Contents: Ferret friends -- Pet profiles -- Ferret firsts -- Life cycle
-- Picking your pet -- Ferret furnishings -- Feasts for ferrets -- Feet
to fur -- Grooming -- Healthy and happy -- Fun with ferrets -- Ferrets
forever -- Pet puzzlers.
  ISBN 1-59036-115-6 (lib. bdg. : alk. paper)
  1. Ferrets as pets--Juvenile literature. [1. Ferrets as pets. 2.
Pets.] I. Title. II. Caring for your pet (Mankato, Minn.)
  SF459.F47H36 2004
  636.9'76628--dc21
                                                     2003001382

                           Printed in the United States of America
                           1 2 3 4 5 6 7 8 9 0   07 06 05 04 03

J
636.976628
48.20
HAM
c.1

Photograph and Text Credits

Every reasonable effort has been made to trace ownership and to obtain permission to reprint copyright material. The publishers would be pleased to have any errors or omissions brought to their attention so that they may be corrected in subsequent printings.

Cover: sable ferret kit (Norvia Behling/Behling and Johnson); **Brandon A. Barnett**: page 10 top; **Norvia Behling/Behling and Johnson**: title page, pages 6 left, 6 middle, 10 bottom, 11 bottom, 15, 18/19; **Gerry Bucsis & Barbara Somerville**: pages 5, 8, 12, 14, 16, 17 left, 20, 21, 22, 23, 24, 25, 26, 28, 30; **Diane Calkins/Click the Photo connection**: pages 7 right, 13, 31; **Corel Corporation**: page 9; **Digital Stock Corporation**: page 17 right; **Eyewire, Inc.**: page 4; **Lawanda Hartman**: pages 3, 6 right, 7 left, 7 middle, 11 top, 27.

Locate the ferret paw prints throughout the book to find useful tips on caring for your pet.

Contents

Ferret Friends

One minute a ferret will play hide-and-seek inside the sleeve of your coat. The next minute he will hide your sock. Ferrets have a reputation for being lively and **mischievous**. Some love to snuggle. Most are playful. They enjoy chewing, digging, bouncing, tugging, and chasing other ferrets. These furry animals are curious, too. They love to explore and can find their way into some very small places.

A ferret would not last long in the wild. Dangers outside the home include cold or hot weather, starvation, **predators**, and disease.

Parents should watch young children who are playing with a ferret to ensure they are properly handling the animal.

A pet ferret will keep you busy. Your ferret will rely on you to keep his cage clean and to provide food and fresh water. You may want to train your ferret to use a litter box. Your ferret will want to run around inside the house for several hours each day. A pet ferret needs to be supervised while he is outside of his cage. Owners need to be sure their home is always a safe, healthy, and happy place for their ferret. Owning a ferret is a big responsibility, but it can be very rewarding to share your home with such a playful friend.

▪ Children may need an adult's help caring for their ferret.

Fascinating Facts

- It is estimated that there are 8 to 10 million pet ferrets in the United States.
- Ferrets have become the third most popular **mammal** pet in the U.S., following cats and dogs.
- Ferrets are intelligent and can learn tricks.
- Ferrets have a musky smell. Like a skunk, they can also give off an odor. The smell is not as strong and does not last as long as a skunk's scent.

Pet Profiles

Ferrets are very social and active animals. A young ferret may need to be trained. An aging ferret will play, but for shorter periods of time. Ferrets' coats come in a variety of colors and patterns. Some ferrets have white feet called mitts. Others have markings on their head or patches on their knees. Sable ferrets are the most common pets.

SABLE

- Dark brown **guard hairs**
- White, cream, beige, or golden **undercoat**
- Brown or black eyes
- Brown or black nose that may be speckled or have a T-shaped pattern
- Raccoon-like markings on the face
- Dark legs and tail

ALBINO

- White or cream guard hairs and undercoat
- Lack of special dyes in the body, called pigments, results in a white coat
- Red eyes
- Pink nose
- Also known as the red-eyed white

CINNAMON

- Reddish-brown guard hairs
- White, beige, or golden undercoat
- Burgundy eyes
- Reddish-brown, light brown, or pink nose that may have a T-shaped pattern
- Does not usually have heavy markings on the face

Both female and male ferrets can make wonderful pets. Males are larger and heavier than females. A female has a thinner, more pointed nose. **Neutered** males are less odorous and more friendly than those who have not been neutered. Fur color does not influence a ferret's **temperament**. Each ferret is born with a unique personality. A ferret's behavior is affected by the way she is treated and trained.

CHOCOLATE

- Milk or chocolate brown guard hairs
- Undercoat is white or golden
- Dark burgundy or brown eyes
- Reddish-brown, beige, or pink nose that may have a light brown, T-shaped pattern

SILVER MITT

- White guard hairs mixed with some darker strands
- Has white or off-white undercoat
- Dark burgundy eyes
- White feet
- May have a white patch on the chest called a bib
- Markings on the face are not as heavy as seen on other ferret varieties, such as the sable

BUTTERSCOTCH

- Butterscotch guard hairs
- White, beige, or golden undercoat
- Lighter version of the sable ferret
- Like most ferrets, the tail, ears, and legs are darker than the rest of the body
- Butterscotch-colored nose
- Once known as the Siamese ferret

Ferret Firsts

There is some mystery about when ferrets were first **domesticated**. Some experts believe that ferrets were first domesticated more than 2,500 years ago—before cats. Some people believe Egyptians were the first people to keep ferrets. Others believe Greeks were the first to domesticate the animal. Romans used ferrets to chase rabbits from burrows. The rabbits were captured for food. Over several centuries, this hunting method reached Great Britain and other European countries.

■ Ferrets are domestic animals. They cannot survive in nature.

Three hundred years ago, ferrets were used to catch rats on ships sailing to the United States. In Spain in the 1870s, ferrets were also used to catch and kill rodents. Some farmers felt ferrets were pests, and some hunters did not like competing with ferrets for **prey**. In the 1900s, rodent populations were controlled by chemicals. This replaced the need for ferrets. As a result, many places made it illegal to own a ferret.

Ferrets have since become a popular pet. Most places have again made it legal to own a ferret. **Breeders** raise ferrets to meet the growing demand. Some **veterinarians** specialize in ferrets. There are ferret clubs and organizations. Some ferrets are even shown in competitions.

Check local game commission laws to learn if pet ferrets are legal in your state, city, or area. You may need to get a permit to adopt a ferret.

Fascinating Facts

- The ferret is a member of the *Mustelidae* family. Ferrets are related to badgers, minks, sea otters, skunks, and weasels.
- Both Queen Elizabeth I and Queen Victoria of England owned ferrets. Queen Victoria gave ferrets as gifts.
- Ferret breeding became so important in New London, Ohio, that the town became known as "Ferretville."

Life Cycle

Most people buy their ferret friend from an animal shelter, a pet store, or a breeder. Baby ferrets can be adopted when they are about 8 weeks old. Some people choose older ferrets. Knowing about the stages of your ferret's life will help you understand and care for your ferret.

Newborn Ferrets

A mother ferret usually gives birth to five or six babies, or kits, at one time. Newborn kits are about 2 inches long. Their eyes are closed and their skin is pink. They appear to be hairless, but they are actually covered with fine hairs. The mother is very protective of her kits and will stay close by.

Senior Ferrets

As early as 4 years old, ferrets' fur starts to thin and turn white or gray. Their eyesight may begin to weaken. Older ferrets will want to take more naps and snuggle more often. Senior ferrets sometimes develop dental problems or arthritis. Extra trips to the veterinarian may be needed.

Fascinating Facts

- The average life span of a ferret is between 6 and 10 years.
- A senior ferret's paw pads sometimes become dry. Rubbing them with petroleum jelly or vitamin E cream can help keep them moist.
- Ferrets need to sleep between 15 and 20 hours each day.

First Weeks

As kits mature, they develop a thick, white coat. Except for albinos, kits' hair will darken. Between 3 and 4 weeks of age, their eyes open. They are ready to begin eating soft, mushy food. At 5 weeks old, their coats are thick and full. By about 6 weeks of age, they are ready to be **weaned** from their mother's milk.

Adults

Ferrets have finished growing by about 6 months of age. An adult female, or jill, weighs 1 to 3 pounds. Jills grow up to 18 inches long, including their tail. An adult male, or hob, weighs 3 to 5 pounds. Hobs grow up to 24 inches long. Female ferrets can give birth within their first year. Jills that are not bred must be **spayed** by 5 or 6 months of age.

Picking Your Pet

When you look at the bright-eyed face of a ferret, it is easy to understand why they are popular pets. As adorable as they are, ferrets can be demanding. Think about these questions before you buy a ferret friend.

Kits should not be taken from their mother until they are at least 8 weeks old.

Can I Make My Home Ferret-Friendly?

Ferrets can enter furnace ducts and appliances. They can crawl inside a couch. Ferret owners must block all openings larger than 1 or 2 inches. Cabinet doors should be tightly shut. Objects such as pencil erasers can block a ferret's intestines if eaten. Cleansers, plants, and electrical wiring must be moved out of their reach, too. Ferrets can get along with cats and dogs, but they must be closely watched.

■ Ferrets love to dig, so be sure to protect houseplants by covering the soil with large stones.

Can I Afford a Ferret?

The average cost of a ferret from a pet store or breeder is between $100 and $150. Buying a ferret from a shelter is usually less expensive. Your ferret will need a cage and accessories. Having your ferret spayed or neutered will cost even more. Food, litter, yearly check-ups, and **vaccinations** are regular expenses.

■ Ferrets love to hide their toys. They will also hide keys, remote controls, and socks.

Will I Be a Responsible Owner?

You must be on constant alert, checking that your house is ferret-proofed. Your ferret will depend on you for everything. He will need to play with you for at least 2 hours every day.

Fascinating Facts

- Lost and rescued ferrets are often taken to ferret shelters. A shelter will care for the ferret until someone adopts him.
- Ferrets should not share a home with rodents, birds, fish, or snakes.
- Ferrets love to play with each other, but they may need time to adjust to new roommates.

Ferret Furnishings

Your ferret needs to stay in a cage at night and while you are away. Wire cages are well **ventilated** and make a good home for a pet ferret. Sides measuring 2 to 3 feet should provide enough space for two ferrets. You will need to have a larger cage if you own more ferrets. A two-level cage allows distance between the litter box, food, and sleeping areas. The door should have a secure latch.

■ Ferrets should be kept inside their cage when they are not being watched. Ferrets also need plenty of playtime away from their cage.

A blanket or towel on the cage floor will protect your ferret's feet. It also makes a cozy place for your ferret to sleep. Ferrets prefer their litter box to be placed in a corner. Its sides should be about 3 inches high. One side should be lower so your ferret can enter and exit easily. A light layer of litter inside the litter box keeps it from becoming a fun place for your ferret to play.

Other supplies needed to raise a pet ferret include claw clippers and ferret shampoo. A variety of toys will keep your ferret busy and interested. Ferrets love to tunnel. Tubes made from a dryer hose or cut-off pant legs are ferret favorites. Toys should be made of non-toxic materials without loose or breakable parts that might be accidentally swallowed. You also need a leash and a harness if you want to take your ferret for a walk outdoors.

Ferrets like to dig. Be sure to ferret-proof your house and place plants out of reach before letting your ferret run free inside the house.

■ Ferrets love to chew, so they need toys that do not break easily. Cat toys or hard rubber toys work well.

Fascinating Facts

• Be careful what you use for litter. Some ferrets are allergic to wood chips and shavings. Some cat litters are too dusty or clump, clogging your ferret's nose. Dust-free litter, paper, or wood pellets are good options.

Feasts for Ferrets

There are foods made especially for ferrets. Some owners feed their ferret a high-quality, dry cat food instead of ferret food. In all cases, be sure the food provides a good source of animal protein and animal fat. Soft cat food and dog food do not provide the nutrition that ferrets need. A ferret veterinarian or a ferret breeder can offer advice about the best brands of food. Your ferret may be fussy about the food he eats. Offering your ferret variety will help him become familiar with several kinds of food. Be sure to provide a constant supply of fresh water, too.

It is dangerous to feed chicken or turkey bones to your ferret. Small pieces of bone may block your ferret's intestines.

■ Introduce new foods to your ferret in small amounts. This allows your pets to become used to the food. It may also prevent him from becoming ill.

Ferrets need to eat every 3 to 4 hours. Their food bowls should never be empty. If you feed your pet high-quality food, he will probably not need to take vitamins. Certain vitamins can be fed to your ferret as a treat. Always ask a veterinarian for advice and follow directions.

As a special treat, you can feed your ferret cooked chicken or beef, bananas, raisins, and smooth peanut butter. Be very careful about the type and number of treats you give to your ferret. Otherwise, your ferret may not receive the nutrition she needs to be healthy.

■ Wet food spoils quickly. Be sure to throw out any uneaten food every day.

Fascinating Facts

- Eating hard food helps to keep a ferret's teeth clean. This is because plaque is rubbed off while they eat.
- Kits that are being weaned need to have their food softened with water. They are usually ready for hard food by 3 to 4 months of age.
- Ferrets do not digest sugary foods or nuts well. Chocolate, dairy products, garlic, and onions should also be avoided.
- Ferrets digest their food too quickly to draw enough nutrients from vegetables. Eating too many fruits and vegetables may give your ferret diarrhea.

Feet to Fur

Ferrets are energetic and their bodies are quite flexible. They are also intelligent. Many other physical characteristics make them skilled at hunting and exploring. It is not surprising that such athletic animals love to play.

A ferret's head is long and flat on the top. This shape is well-suited for running through small spaces.

A ferret's backbone is longer than most mammals. It is also very flexible. This helps the ferret to twist and turn when tunneling and running.

Thick, soft fur covers a ferret's body, legs, feet, and head. A ferret may shed some hair, usually in autumn before growing their thick, winter coat. She may shed again in spring. Scent glands found all over the ferret's body give the fur its musky scent.

A ferret's backbone extends into the tail. The tail has about eighteen bones. The hair on a ferret's tail will stand on end when she is excited or frightened. Too much hair loss on the tail may be a sign of illness.

A ferret's eyes are placed slightly to the side and top of the head. This allows them to view a large area. Ferrets can see objects that are close best. They can also see well in shadowy areas. Ferrets have a keen sense of hearing and an excellent sense of smell.

Like humans, ferrets grow two sets of teeth. Baby teeth begin to appear when they are as young as 3 weeks old. Within 2 to 3 months, their permanent teeth have grown. As ferrets grow older, their teeth may become transparent and begin to yellow. This is one way to tell the age of a ferret.

Ferrets' short legs allow them to explore tight places. Their legs are also strong. This allows ferrets to jump, climb, and run. Ferrets have five toes on each foot. Their claws are useful for grasping and digging.

■ SABLE

Fluffing Ferrets

Ferrets groom themselves. To help control odor, you will need to keep your pet's cage clean and change his bedding. If your ferret has been into something messy, he may need a bath. Bathe your ferret in a basin or a bathtub filled with a few inches of lukewarm water. Special ferret shampoos are available. Be careful not to get soap in your ferret's eyes. Rinse your ferret with clean, warm water, and dry him thoroughly.

Running water can frighten your pet. Filling the bathtub before you place your ferret inside creates a calmer bath time.

■ Use a soft brush when grooming your ferret to avoid scratching his skin.

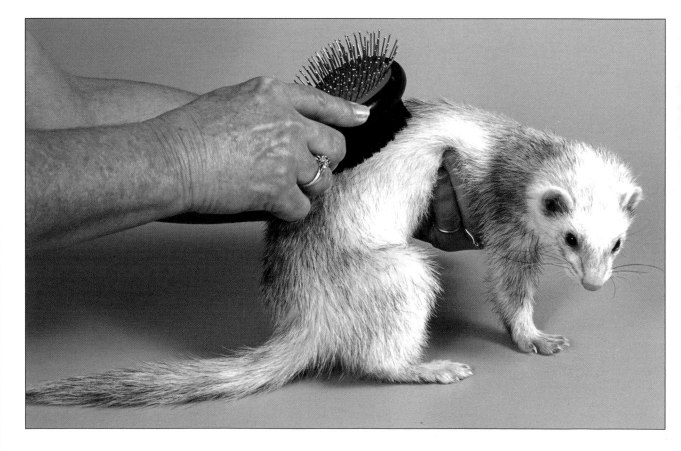

Clean your ferret's ears with a cotton swab at least once each month. Special ear cleansers are available. Do not try to clean inside the ear canal because this can damage your pet's eardrum.

When a ferret's nails are too long, they can become caught in bedding or carpet. Nails should be clipped every 1 to 2 weeks. Either human nail or cat claw clippers will work. Many ferrets do not like having their claws clipped. It is a good idea to ask for an adult's help. Clipping a nail too far down may cause bleeding and pain. If you accidentally clip your ferret's claws too low, a special powder is available to stop the bleeding.

■ Be careful not to squeeze your ferret when grooming or clipping his nails. You might hurt him or cause him stress.

Fascinating Facts

- Like humans, ferrets can have tooth decay and cavities. Your veterinarian can check and clean your ferret's teeth.
- Frequent bathing removes oils from a ferret's skin. The ferret's body will try to replace the oils, resulting in a stronger, musky odor.

Healthy and Happy

Count on your veterinarian to answer questions, give your ferret yearly checkups, treat illnesses, and provide vaccinations to prevent diseases. Not all veterinarians are experienced with ferrets. A local ferret shelter may be able to help you find a veterinarian in your area.

Just like cats, ferrets get hairballs. These clumps of hair can block their intestines. Ask your veterinarian to suggest a product to help prevent hairballs. Ferrets can also get ear infections. Black, heavy ear wax is a sign of **ear mites**. Ferrets easily catch ear mites from other ferrets. A veterinarian can give ferret owners special drops to help get rid of these pests. Unlike most other animals, ferrets can catch a cold or the flu from humans. Try to stay away from your ferret when you are ill. If you must handle your ferret, wash your hands first, and do not cough or sneeze nearby.

Ferrets can catch fleas. Dog flea remedies can be poisonous to ferrets. Ask your veterinarian for advice.

■ It is important to clean your ferret's ears on a regular basis. This will prevent ear mites and infection.

Ferret owners will become more familiar with their pet's behavior and appearance over time. Some signs of illness include changes in her appetite or bathroom habits, weight loss or gain, heavy hair loss, lumps, increased scratching, and extreme sleepiness. By providing your ferret with proper nutrition, veterinary care, exercise, and a safe environment, many health problems can be prevented.

■ A ferret should visit the veterinarian for a thorough checkup at least once each year.

Fascinating Facts

- If the temperature is hotter than 80 degrees Fahrenheit, your ferret can become ill. Panting and limpness are two signs that your ferret is not feeling well. You can avoid problems by keeping her cool with a fan or by giving her cool water. Never leave your ferret in a hot car.

Fun with Ferrets

Your ferret will need time to adjust to his new home. You should approach your pet slowly and speak quietly. To hold your ferret, support his chest and front legs with one hand and his behind with your other hand. It is also safe to hold your ferret by the loose skin at the back of the neck, called the scruff. You should always support your ferret's bottom. Holding your ferret either of these two ways should make him feel safe and relaxed.

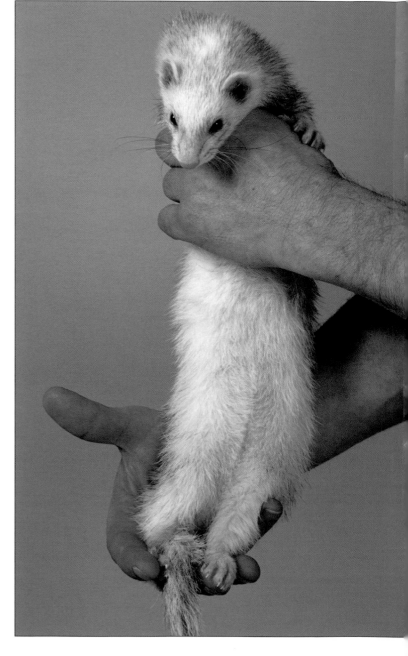

■ Ferrets need to be held properly to prevent injuring their fragile spines.

Pet Peeves

Ferrets do not like:
- loud noises
- closed doors
- being held still
- dusty cat litter
- bitter apple flavor
- being too hot

Ferrets can be trained to use a litter box. To train him, put your ferret in the litter box every half hour. Leave a bit of waste in the litter box to remind your ferret of its purpose.

Just like puppies, ferrets need to be taught how to play nicely. You can train your ferret not to nip by picking him up by the scruff and sternly saying "no." You can also spray a bitter apple flavor on your hands to discourage your ferret from biting. Ferrets do not like the taste of this spray.

Ferrets are smart and enjoy attention. They like to play chasing games and tug-of-war. A ferret can also be trained to answer to his or her name and perform tricks such as rolling over and sitting up. Treats are a positive way to encourage good behavior.

One or more litter boxes in corners around your ferret's play area will help prevent accidents.

■ Put a litter box in every room where your ferret is let out to play.

Fascinating Facts

• If an area smells like a litter box, a ferret will use it like one. Accident spots should be thoroughly cleaned with safe cleansers.

Ferrets Forever

Ferrets have helped humans for thousands of years. Today, ferrets are used for medical research. Sometimes they are used to study the flu or the effects of different medicines.

Ferrets are well known for their expert tunneling abilities. Specially trained ferrets are often sent to do work in spaces that are too small for humans. Ferrets have been used to string telephone wire underground and pull cables through oil pipelines. These ferrets wear small harnesses attached to wires and cables. At the other end of the tunnel, the ferrets receive tasty rewards for their work. In London, England, a team of ferrets helped connect cables for television broadcasts of millennium celebrations.

Ferrets can be trained to walk on a leash.

Fascinating Facts

- Black-footed ferrets are wild ferrets that live in the United States. The population of their main food source, the prairie dog, has decreased. As a result, these ferrets have become **endangered**. To help increase the population, scientists have been capturing and breeding black-footed ferrets and releasing them into nature.

Ferrets have appeared in many books, movies, and television shows.

People are fascinated by ferrets. Web sites and publications such as *Modern Ferret Magazine* are devoted especially to ferrets. Ferrets have also appeared in television shows and movies. Richard Bach has written a set of fiction books about ferrets. Bach is the author of the book *Jonathan Livingston Seagull*. He has several pet ferrets. This series of books features the adventures of ferret characters who are involved in rescue missions.

Ferret Tales

Ferrets are the subject of a few of *Aesop's Fables*. "The Snake, the House-Ferret, and the Mice" is about two mice who get caught in the middle of a fight between a snake and a ferret. The timid mice come out of hiding while the ferret and the snake are fighting. When the ferret and the snake see the mice, they stop fighting and attack the mice instead. The moral of the story is that those who get involved in other people's fights may become victims of the fight.

Taken from *Aesop's Fables*.

Pet Puzzlers

What do you know about ferrets? If you can answer the following questions correctly, you may be ready to own a pet ferret.

Q How much sleep does a ferret need?

A healthy ferret will sleep between 15 and 20 hours a day. Between sleeps, ferrets enjoy plenty of activity. Changes in sleep patterns and extreme sleepiness may be signs of illness.

Q How do I ferret-proof my home?

Plan ahead and remove dangers in the home. Block all small gaps that are larger than 1 or 2 inches. Put dangerous items out of reach. Watch your ferret when she is out of her cage.

Q Does my ferret need a friend?

Ferrets enjoy each other's company, but a single ferret can be quite content, too. Dogs and cats can get along with a ferret, but other pets, such as rodents, birds, snakes, and fish do not. Your ferret will be happiest if you play with her for at least 2 hours every day.

Q How often does a ferret need to eat?

A ferret needs to eat every 3 to 4 hours. A ferret's food bowl should never be empty.

Q How can I train my ferret not to nip?

You can train your ferret not to nip by saying a firm "no" while holding her by the scruff. You can also spray a bitter apple scent on your hands.

Q Is it normal for a ferret to lose hair?

A ferret may shed in the spring and again in the fall. A ferret's hair may also thin out as she ages. If a ferret is losing unusual amounts of hair, it may mean that she is ill.

Q When should a ferret be spayed or neutered?

Male and female ferrets should be spayed or neutered by 5 or 6 months of age.

Ferret Fame

Before you buy your pet ferret, write down some ferret names that you like. Some names may work better for a female ferret. Others may suit a male ferret. Here are just a few suggestions:

Feisty

Cuddles

Slinky

Digger

Chuckles

Bandit

Petunia

Franklin

Columbus

Felicity

Frequently Asked Questions

My ferret makes sounds. What do they mean?

When a ferret makes a clucking or "dook-dook" sound, it usually means he is happy and energized. Ferrets hiss out of fear and when they fight or play-fight. If your ferret makes a screeching sound, it might mean he is frightened or hurt.

Can I take my ferret on a trip?

If you plan to take your ferret on a trip, ensure your pet will be safe and comfortable. You will need to use a secure pet carrier for airplane and car rides. You must also provide litter, food, and water. Check ahead with the airline, the government, and the hotel for travel regulations.

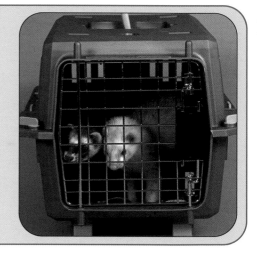

What is normal ferret behavior?

Owners may be startled if their ferret is jumping about wildly and banging into things. Actually, this is a sign of a happy, fun-loving ferret. A ferret often shivers when he is excited or shortly after waking. Ferrets shiver when they are trying to get warm. They also sneeze once in a while. Ferrets will sometimes lick at soap or other substances. If done in small amounts, this is not dangerous.

More Information

Animal Organizations

You can help ferrets stay healthy and happy by learning more about them. Many organizations are dedicated to teaching people how to care for and protect their pet pals. For more ferret information, write to the following organizations:

The American Ferret Association, Inc.
PMB 255
626-C Admiral Dr.
Annapolis, MD 21401

STAR*Ferrets (Shelters That
Adopt and Rescue Ferrets)
P.O. Box 1832
Springfield, VA 22151-0832

Web Sites

To answer more of your ferret questions, go online and surf to the following Web sites:

Ferret Central
www.ferretcentral.org

The Ferret Owner's Manual
www.thechipster.com/fert-man.html

VetCentric
www.vetcentric.com

Words to Know

breeders: people who raise and sell animals

domesticated: tamed, not wild

ear mites: small bugs that live inside an animal's ears

endangered: animals whose populations are so low they are in danger of disappearing completely

guard hairs: long, stiff hairs

mammal: warm-blooded animal with a backbone and hair, whose young are fed with their mother's milk

mischievous: naughty

Mustelidae: family of furry animals with long bodies and short legs

neutered: an operation that makes males unable to reproduce

predators: animals that hunt and eat other animals

prey: animals that are hunted and eaten by other animals

spayed: an operation that makes females unable to reproduce

temperament: personality

undercoat: soft, fine, short hair

vaccinations: medicines given to help prevent diseases and illnesses

ventilated: provided clean, fresh air in an enclosed space

veterinarians: animal doctors

weaned: becoming used to food other than a mother's milk

Index